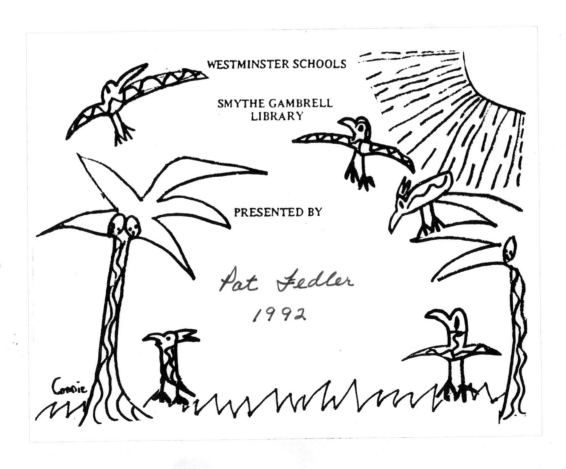

WESTMINSTER SCHOOLS

SMYTHE GAMBRELL
LIBRARY

PRESENTED BY

Pat Fedler
1992

To our children
Betty Ann, Rick, and Pat
who taught us to see the beauty of mathematics
through the eyes of a child

John and Stacey Wahl
Ridgefield, Connecticut

Second edition

Library of Congress Cataloging in Publication Data:

Wahl, John.
I can count the petals of a flower.

Summary: Introduces the numbers one through sixteen and some basic mathematical concepts using the petals of a variety of flowers.

1. Counting—Juvenile literature. 2. Flowers—Pictorial works—Juvenile literature. [1. Counting. 2. Flowers—Pictorial works] I. Wahl, Stacey. II. Title.

QA113.W33   1985   513'.2   85-13670
ISBN 0-87353-224-4

ABOUT THE BOOK

The book began to grow in 1969. My husband, John, had unusual success growing wild flowers in our back woods. With a fine new camera, acquired for our twenty-fifth wedding anniversary, he began photographing the development of wild flowers as they emerged in the spring. The pictures recorded the exquisite delicate detail that a viewer seldom observes from normal eye height.

Photographing wild flowers on trips became a new hobby. Then one day a young child was looking at a picture of a native Colorado flower, the oxeye. She happily announced that it had fifteen petals! As a teacher of mathematics teachers, I realized that she had opened a new approach to a needed mathematical skill. The title for this new project was obviously *I Can Count the Petals of a Flower.*

We had blithely supposed that it would be a simple task to find flowers with petals representing all the counting numbers through sixteen. Some were easy to find—but to find a seven-petaled flower? After considerable searching, we asked questions and researched flower books. The results were discouraging. Progress came to a standstill. Then we had a lucky break. Our newspaper announced that Harold William Rickett was to give a talk on wild flowers in Roxbury, Connecticut. We already owned and enjoyed his beautiful *Wild Flowers of the United States—the Northeastern States.* Naturally we attended the lecture and waited to ask our own special question, "Are there any seven-petaled flowers?" I

shall always remember my happiness when he replied, "Oh yes, there is one. I have it on page 301 of my book. It is very small and grows near Roxbury in the early spring. It is called *Trientalis borealis,* a starflower." Once again the book seemed a possibility.

Meanwhile, as a teacher of teachers, I was aware of the increasing number of children who were having trouble with their times tables. Counting petals of flowers promised a fresh approach to these problems of learning primes and composites and evens and odds. A new section of the book began to take shape, picturing, for example, three flowers with four petals and four flowers with three petals. The task of finding these flowers at a proper camera angle for countability became a fun-filled challenge.

A new problem presented itself. To allow for all the factors, we would need eight different sets of pictures of two-petaled flowers. Flower books indicated there was a species of impatiens that had two petals. Unfortunately, all those in our area had two large petals and two tiny ones. The temptation to solve our problem by removing the two tiny petals was great. However, one does not cheat a child!

Luckily I remembered a picture John had taken at our daughter's Peace Corps home in Chandigarh, India. It had four flowers with two petals each and was called the crown of thorns. Once again luck was with us in discovering a beautiful "solace garden" behind a funeral home in Danbury, Connecticut. Mr. Hull, the owner, graciously gave us permission to photograph his full-flowering crown of thorns for our eight sets of two-petaled flowers. Others of his beautiful flowers also appear in the book.

Serious health problems postponed our search for flowers until the following spring. With John's health restored and an added appreciation of life, we set out one day in May to look for the seven-petaled starflower. We searched for hours to no avail. As the sun was lowering in the sky, we got lost on a newly developed road. One place was steep and rocky and damp. I instinctively asked John to back up to that spot. We got out and looked around, and I found a species of flower my husband had never photographed. As I stood still to hold that location, my eyes adapted to the environment. There at my feet were plants with tiny white flowers, and sure enough, when I counted them, they had seven petals—our starflowers! We have found other seven-petaled flowers since, but the starflower remains special to us.

The thirteen-petaled flower surprises many viewers, but thirteen petals is common in members of the daisy family. Eleven and fourteen became the elusive ones. Neighbors, colleagues, and former students began counting petals for us. (They report that it has now become a habit.) The eleven-petaled Thumbelina was found at a local plant nursery.

Fourteen petals became the new obsession. It seemed impossible to find. One day, again by instinct, I went to a plant nursery in an adjoining state. There, a gentleman was in the process of purchasing six flowerpots of yellow daisies. There in his collection was one beautiful yellow daisy with fourteen petals! Since he was in the process of buying the plants, I offered to buy that one plant at double the price, explaining my urgent need for the flower. The proprietor was annoyed by this and told me to go down to his basic supply and find another. I hurriedly counted all the daisies, and there was not a fourteen-petaled flower among them. I rushed back, explaining the situation and again asked to buy that plant that was so important to me. In extreme annoyance, the proprietor went down to his basic supply to prove me wrong. He counted all the petals and had to come back and admit that he was wrong. Luckily, the purchaser (bless him!) had become interested in this unusual situation and had awaited the proprietor's verdict. He then willingly let me buy the special plant—and at the regular price, too. Thanks to him, many people can enjoy the picture, and it is one of the prettiest in the book.

In the meantime I began testing young children's reactions to the book. They loved it! Thanks to "Sesame Street," these preschoolers could count. However, they presented a new problem by asking, "What kind of flower is this?" No adult wants to be unable to answer a questioning child, so we now had the new task of identifying the correct name for each flower.

An additional dimension of the book presented itself. For many years I have found the Cuisenaire rods a valuable teaching tool. They are small, color-coded rods with each color representing a given number—if the white rod is called one, then the red rod represents two, and so on. We already had a white calla for one and a red flower for two—could we possibly be lucky enough to find other flowers color coded to the rods? We succeeded with light green for three, purple for four, yellow for five, and orange for ten. Seven being black and eight being brown were impossible, and so we had to settle for white ones. Could there possibly be a green six-petaled flower? Green flowers are very scarce—and to find a green six-petaled one? In England I found a few bushes with green five-petaled flowers. I counted and counted, but they were all consistently five petaled. However, the elusive hope for finding one remained.

In 1974 while visiting Mount Rainier in Washington, we were enjoying a view from the edge of a snowbank. Suddenly I shouted, "John, I have found my six-petaled green flower!" You can imagine the looks on the faces of the people who heard my shouts. Their looks didn't matter to me—I had found it! Alas! John did not have his close-up lens along, and the floret was very tiny; also we were in a national park, and the rule is *Don't pick the flowers!* I went to the rangers' headquarters and explained my plight— how I had looked for two whole years and how it was a special book for children and how of all things my husband didn't have the right lens along. The ranger was skeptical, but the young hikers waiting for hiking permits were all on my side. The ranger called the head ranger and let me plead my case. The head ranger agreed that I could take one frond from the plant. The hikers found some plastic, and we carefully wrapped the Indian poke in snow for the return trip to Seattle.

It was after our return to Seattle that I realized that the special lens had been left, not in Seattle, but a continent away in Ridgefield, Connecticut. John had tried his best to get a picture without the right equipment, but to play it safe we carefully nursed the frond via Amtrak across the country to the correct camera lens. The Indian poke obligingly fought for survival until its picture was taken and then gave in to the inevitable wilting. Now—has anyone been able to find a nine-petaled blue flower? I am still looking.

So there is the story of our book. With fun, persistence, help from others, and just plain luck, the book has been finished. Every flower was photographed in its natural beauty. I hope it can become a special resource book for children who are learning mathematics.

The fun we had together producing the book is a reward in itself. I had often thought of it as a special grandparents' book to be enjoyed with a child curled up in the grandparent's lap sharing the enjoyment of the beauty and the color. Then we found that our names would be changed to Grandpa and Grandma. Now all the love that was put into the book for other children can be enjoyed by our own grandchildren.

Stacey Wahl

Count My Petals

White calla lily

1

Crown of thorns

2

Snowdrop

3

Clematis

4

Fringed loosestrife

5

Indian poke

Starflower

Bloodroot

Windflower

9

Golden flower of the Incas

10

Let's Count Again

Lily of the Nile

1

Crown of thorns

2

Wake-robin

3

Chinese dogwood

Crown of thorns

4

Wild flax

5

Yellow day lily

Painted trillium

Crown of thorns

6

Sweet bell pepper

7

Clematis

Celandine

Crown of thorns

8

Tickseed

Spiderwort

9

White columbine

Deptford pink

Crown of thorns

10

Thumbelina

11

Liverleaf

Spiderwort

Black-eyed Susan

Crown of thorns

Chinese dogwood

12

Cineraria

13

Starflower

Boston yellow daisy

Crown of thorns

14

Bridal veil

Colorado oxeye

15

Deptford pink

Pink dogwood

White Marguerite

Tickseed

16

Crown of thorns

Now...

Peace lily

Musk mallow

Dayflower

Sundrops

Butterfly lily

I Have?

Clematis

Trout lily

Bloodroot

Rue anemone

Hybrid dahlia

Red trillium

Crown of thorns

Tulip tree

Clematis

Common violet

Black-eyed Susan

Painter's palette

Bunchberry

Left Out?

Houseleek

Cineraria

Passionflower

Coreopsis

Black-eyed Susan

Greek anemone

Count Carefully for a Surprise!

Starflower

Browallia

Clematis

Clematis

Mock orange

Sweet bell pepper

HOW TO USE THE BOOK

Our book was planned to help children enjoy the pleasures of counting the petals of a flower. Each photograph has captured the exquisite beauty of flowers just as they occur in nature. Each is identified so the child's question, "What kind of flower is it?" can be answered.

For younger children, the book introduces or reinforces the counting experiences they enjoy at an early age. The first page shows a flower with one petal, and the child should say, "One." The second page shows a flower with two petals, and the child should count, "One, two" and recognize that there are two petals. Counting around in a circle may be a new experience; so the child should be encouraged to keep track of the first petal counted, perhaps by holding a finger on it.

Younger children can use the entire book just for counting. For older children, the counting experiences lead into new and different insights of mathematical concepts. Though the book was designed for "guided discovery," some children will need helpful hints from an adult to discover all its mathematical ideas. The teacher will recognize that some of these concepts include evens and odds, factors (multiplication facts), primes and composites, and examples of line and point symmetry.

In the review section, the numerals have been left out. First, there is a section where the flowers are arranged in sequence so the younger child can be successful. In the next section there are omissions; children are challenged to find the number of petals on the missing flower. In the last part, the photographs record a surprising botanical phenomenon. The child who counts very carefully will discover the surprise.

We hope you and the children will enjoy this book.

John and Stacey Wahl

BOTANICAL NAMES OF THE FLOWERS

Black-eyed Susan	*Rudbeckia serotina* / *Rudbeckia hirta*
Bloodroot	*Sanguinaria canadensis*
Boston yellow daisy	*Chrysanthemum frutescens*
Bridal veil	*Tradescantia minutiae*
Browallia	*Browallia americana*
Bunchberry	*Cornus canadensis*
Butterfly lily	*Calochortus gunnisonii*
Celandine	*Chelidonium majus*
Chinese dogwood	*Cornus kousa*
Cineraria	*Senecio cruentus*
Clematis	*Clematis* / *Clematis jackmanii* / *Clematis lanuginosa*
Colorado oxeye	*Helianthus annus*
Common violet	*Viola papilionacea*
Coreopsis	*Coreopsis maritimi*
Crown of thorns	*Euphorbia milii*
Dayflower	*Commelina communis*
Deptford pink	*Dianthus armeria*
Fringed loosestrife	*Steironema ciliata*
Golden flower of the Incas	*Tithonia rotundifolia*
Greek anemone	*Anemone blanda*
Houseleek	*Sempervivum arachoinideum*
Hybrid dahlia	*Dahlia mignon*
Indian poke	*Veratrum viride*
Lily of the Nile	*Zantedeschia aethiopica*
Liverleaf	*Hepatica americana*
Mock orange	*Philadelphus coronarius*
Musk mallow	*Malva moschata*
Painted trillium	*Trillium undulatum*
Painter's palette	*Anthurium andraeanum*
Passionflower	*Passiflora violacea*
Peace lily	*Spathiphyllum walissi*

Pink dogwood	*Cornus florida rubra*	Thumbelina	*Zinnia haugeanea*
Red trillium	*Trillium erectum*	Trout lily	*Erythronium americanum*
Rue anemone	*Anemonella thalictroides*	Tulip tree	*Liriodendron tulipifera*
Snowdrop	*Galanthus nivalis*	Wake-robin	*Trillium erectum*
Spiderwort	{ *Tradescantia ohiensis* *Tradescantia virginiana*	White calla	*Zantedeschia aethiopica*
		White columbine	*Aquilegia hybrida*
Starflower	*Trientalis borealis*	White Marguerite	*Chrysanthemum frutescens*
Sundrops	*Oenothera parviflora*	Wild flax	*Linum lewisii*
Sweet bell pepper	*Capsicum innum*	Windflower	*Anemonella thalictroides*
Tickseed	{ *Coreopsis auriculata* *Coreopsis drumondi*	Yellow day lily	*Hemerocallis lilio-asphodelus*

SOME CHILDREN COUNT LIKE THIS

ENGLISH	FRENCH	SPANISH	GERMAN	ITALIAN	HEBREW	HINDI NUMERALS
one	un	uno	eins	uno	ehad	१
two	deux	dos	zwei	due	shenayim	२
three	trois	tres	drei	tre	shelosha	३
four	quatre	cuatro	vier	quattro	arbaa	४
five	cinq	cinco	fünf	cinque	hamisha	५
six	six	seis	sechs	sei	shisha	६
seven	sept	siete	sieben	sette	shiva	७
eight	huit	ocho	acht	otto	shemona	८
nine	neuf	nueve	neun	nove	tisha	९
ten	dix	diez	zehn	dieci	asara	१०
eleven	onze	once	elf	undici	ahad-asar	११
twelve	douze	doce	zwölf	dodici	sheneym-asar	१२
thirteen	treize	trece	dreizehn	tredici	shelosha-asar	१३
fourteen	quatorze	catorce	vierzehn	quattordici	arbaa-asar	१४
fifteen	quinze	quince	fünfzehn	quindici	hamisha-asar	१५
sixteen	seize	dieciseis	sechzehn	sedici	shisha-asar	१६

This hardcover edition is dedicated to the memory of John Wahl.